BRISBANE

Brisbane — Portrait of a City is a comprehensive digest of Queensland's capital city in all of its subtropical splendour. Its texts, pictures and captions give what a very friendly resident would proudly provide in person in a 'show and tell' trip to a first-time visitor. The city's colours from the brown river to the blue skies and from the green forest to the golden sands are reproduced faithfully in an attractive, easy-to-read publication. Sections take an overview of topics such as the Brisbane River, the city and its old and new buildings, the relaxed lifestyle of its residents in the city and its sprawling suburbs, the city and the arts, its essential industry, its place in the world of nature, and of course its surrounds including the famed Gold and Sunshine Coasts and hinterlands.

A special feature of its 320 colour pictures are its panoramic scenes — about as close as modern photographic equipment can get in two dimensions to one pair of eyes. Within its covers lie some of the reasons why Brisbane is the centre of one of the fastest-growing regions in Australia, and why more than 800 000 people call Brisbane home.

BRISBANE

PORTRAIT OF A CITY

Robert Brown and Associates

Published and distributed by
Robert Brown & Associates (Qld) Pty Ltd
7 Atherton Street, Buranda Qld 4102, Australia

© Copyright 1991

Design by Sue Tester

Photography by Keith Wilson — Photographer, Brisbane City Council

Additional texts and captions by Don Marshall

National Library of Australia Registry Card No. and ISBN 1 86273 053 9

The assistance of the Brisbane City Council in the production of
this book is gratefully acknowledged.

Additional photography: Ron Lockens — Just Photography, Brisbane Sports and
Entertainment Complex, Performing Arts Complex, Queensland Museum,
Queensland Tourist and Travel Corporation, The Broncos,
The Bullets Basketball Team.

CONTENTS

FOREWORD

Brisbane is a great City. I'm sure you agree.

It is a city diverse in beauty and rich in its quality of life.

It is a City with a thousand faces, a thousand places – a thousand different pictures.

They say a picture paints a thousand words. The pictures in this book speak volumes.

It has captured the qualities that set Brisbane apart from cities throughout the world.

It takes us on a journey through Brisbane's inner city, its character filled suburbs and along its winding river. It has captured our culture and our way of life.

It paints a portrait of Brisbane as unique as an individual's fingerprint.

It makes me proud to be a part of this City.

That's why I'm committed to working full–time with the people of Brisbane to paint an even greater portrait of our future.

Whether you live in Brisbane or whether you simply want to remember what makes this City special, this book is a masterpiece to be treasured.

Jim Soorley
Lord Mayor of Brisbane

INTRODUCTION

Brisbane is the business centre and capital of Queensland, Australia's 'Sunshine State'. It is a progressive, expanding city with a green, sub-tropical character and an outdoor leisurely lifestyle.

Through a growing appreciation of heritage in recent years, Brisbane has benefited from unprecedented restoration of its older buildings. As a result, the city is a successful blend of old and new, with historic landmarks such as the convict-built Windmill on Wickham Terrace faithfully preserved and standing as part of the backdrop to the city highrise. The development of Brisbane reflects its standing as a world-class city and the lifestyle which each year attracts visitors and new residents alike. Pedestrian malls, outdoor eating places, green courtyards within city buildings and the extension of bicycle ways take advantage of Brisbane's sunshine and the outdoor way of life.

The Brisbane River, its potential for recreation ignored for many years, has taken on a new role in the city. It is now seen as an integral part of the city, and not just a stretch of water to cross by bridge. Commercial developments like the Riverside Centre and Waterfront Place, the paddleboat restaurant Kookaburra Queen and the floating John Oxley Restaurant have brought people back to the river. By international standards, Brisbane is a young city. It was established as a penal settlement in 1825. Yet Brisbane has hosted two of the world's most prestigious events — the Commonwealth Games and a world exposition. The 1982 Commonwealth Games in Brisbane was hailed as 'the friendly games'. It brought the athletes of the Commonwealth nations together in a spirit of friendship and peace, and gave the city the confidence to stage a successful World Expo six years later in 1988. World Expo 88 attracted three million interstate and overseas visitors during its six months. It also gave Brisbane an opportunity to 'show off' to the world and to use a single event as a major catalyst for the development of tourism and investment. Expo 88 was a cultural milestone in Brisbane's development. It introduced Brisbane people to street entertainment on a large scale and brought to the city some of the finest performances and exhibitions ever to tour Australia. The legacy of Expo for Brisbane people has been the growth of the entertainment industry and a greater appreciation of culture. The Brisbane Entertainment Centre, north of the city at Boondall, the imposing Cultural Centre on the city's South Bank and the City Hall Art Gallery and Museum attract exhibitions and performances of world-class standard, confirming the city's growing status as a cultural centre of Australia.

As well as entertainment, Brisbane offers many natural attractions for visitors. The Brisbane River opens into Moreton Bay, one of the most magnificent waterways in Australia. The Bay is dotted with islands and weekend leisure craft, and boasts game fishing and diving on sunken ships among its many tourist activities. Brisbane is the tourist gateway to places like the Gold Coast, less than an hour to the south, and the Sunshine Coast to the north. West of the city is the Darling Downs and Toowoomba, Queensland's 'Garden City'. Rainforests and mountain waterfalls are within a short drive of Brisbane and day-trippers can tour the wine belt around Stanthorpe or the rich farming lands near Nambour. A day's travel from Brisbane will take visitors to the Great Barrier Reef, one of Australia's most precious natural attractions and one of the seven wonders of the world. Head west from the city and the Outback opens vast horizons and special places like Carnarvon Gorge.

Brisbane has become a popular destination for conferences, thanks largely to its visitor appeal. Brisbane was Australia's 'convention city' in 1988 during World Expo, and won the right to stage the Lions International Convention in 1991, bringing the event to the Southern Hemisphere for the first time and giving Brisbane the distinction of hosting the country's largest conference. Conferences mix business and pleasure, and in Brisbane there is a wide range of activities to enjoy. There are cruises which explore the Brisbane River, bus tours to take in the city's interest spots and heritage, Botanic Gardens, weekend festivals and country markets, and a range of restaurants to suit every taste and pocket. Every year in Brisbane, the country comes to town with the 'Ekka'. The Royal National Association exhibition features all the fun of the fair and the best of Queensland's livestock and produce. Warana is Brisbane's Spring Fair when the city becomes caught up in street entertainment, parades, free concerts, fine theatre and a never-ending range of activities for young and old. Modern-day Brisbane spans the river with seven bridges and many commuter ferry services. The highs and lows of the river are recorded in the Queensland Maritime Museum at South Brisbane.

PARKS, PEAKS AND OTHER PLACES

Brisbane has more than 1000 parks and gardens throughout its 1220 sq.km. The oldest is the City Botanic Gardens, established in 1855. It was here that the early settlers experimented with plants and vegetables, and the results are still to be seen in the huge stands of exotic and native palms and flowering trees. New Farm Park, also on the river, is famous for its roses — it has 22 000 bushes — and its avenues of jacaranda and poinciana trees. Another Botanic Gardens stands at the foot of Mt Coot-tha, a showplace of modern landscaping which features a tropical plant and butterfly dome and the Sir Thomas Brisbane Planetarium. A Japanese Garden is a cultural gift from Japan and was transplanted from the site of World Expo 88.

One of the most dominant features of Brisbane is its bushland. Brisbane Forest Park is a 26 500-hectare bushland reserve which extends across the mountains behind the city. It is dotted with picnic facilities and lookouts and among the many activities within BFP are night-time wildlife spotlighting and fossicking for gold in an old mine. Mt Coot-tha is the 'high point' of any visit to Brisbane. The mountain is 285 metres above sea level and affords a panoramic view of most of the city and region, including Moreton Bay. Mt Coot-tha is the Aboriginal name for 'place of wild honey'. Other lookout points include Bartley's Hill to the north (79 metres), Mt Gravatt to the south-east (195 metres), and White's Hill to the east (112 metres).

CIVIC PRIDE

In the 1920s, Brisbane built one of its most controversial buildings, the City Hall. It was the talk of Australia and dubbed the 'million pound hall' because of its then extravagant price tag. It is the only City Hall in Australia, and in spite of losing its one-time status as the city's tallest building, City Hall remains among the best-known civic buildings in the country. Construction took 10 years from 1920. It features Corinthian columns and Ionic collonades, and a 92 metre high clock tower with the largest clock face in Australia. The City Hall also features relief sculptures carved on site by eminent Australian artist Daphne Mayo. She worked in rain, heat and dust behind screens so that the finished work would be a surprise for the people of Brisbane.

Brisbane's architecture is varied. There is the Queensland Cultural Centre, its no-nonsense style in direct contrast to its interior of theatres and exhibition halls. In the suburbs are Brisbane's famous houses, built high on 'stilts' or 'stumps' to catch the Bay breezes and to make the most of the city's often hilly terrain. Parliament House also combines the best of the international and local worlds with French Renaissance styling and Queensland sandstone, cedar and copper. Built in 1891, Parliament House overlooks the City Botanic Gardens on one side and the Brisbane River on the other.

GO SHOPPING

The Queen Street Mall is one of Australia's most successful shopping precincts. Specialty shops and complexes like the Wintergarden and Top of the Mall, Australia's largest retail centre, flank the busy pedestrian thoroughfare. Only minutes from the city heart is Fortitude Valley, an early Brisbane retail centre which today boasts the Chinatown and Brunswick Street shopping malls. In the suburbs, large air-conditioned shopping centres offer a variety of merchandise and convenient shopping.

City and country markets are popular places on weekends. Paddy's Market at Teneriffe opens every day, while on Sunday there is the Cat's Tango Pure Craft Riverside Market in the city and the Pine Rivers Country Market at Petrie.

THE ECHO OF CHAINS

You can almost hear the faint echo of chains in parts of the city. In the 1820s, Brisbane became the address for the worst of the country's convicts. Surveyor General John Oxley discovered the site of Brisbane and in 1823 named the Brisbane River after the then Governor of New South Wales, Major-General Sir Thomas MacDougall Brisbane. The original penal settlement was established at Redcliffe, just north of Brisbane. This was later moved to the present site of Brisbane. Here, the convict settlement spread. The Female Factory Prison was on the site of today's General Post Office and the male prisoners' barracks were in Queen Street between Albert and George Streets. The vegetable gardens later became the City Botanic Gardens and wheat grew where the city's tallest buildings now stand. In 1842 when the area opened to free settlers, Brisbane began a new chapter of development. On 6 June 1859, Queensland separated from New South Wales.

Today, reminders of the early days of settlement, gracious and grim, remain. The city's oldest building is the Windmill on Wickham Terrace built in 1828 by convicts to mill flour. It soon became known as the 'Tower of Torture', as many prisoners died on the treadmill installed when the mill did not work well. As punishment, 14 convicts in irons took 3840 steps every hour from sunrise to dusk. The old Commissariat Stores in William Street overlooking the river is another reminder of Brisbane's history. It was built in 1829 and over the years has been a storehouse, customs house and a shelter for immigrants. It is now the headquarters of the Royal Historical Society of Queensland. The Treasury Building at the corner of Queen and George Streets dates from 1885 and stands on the site of the convict settlement's officers' quarters and military barracks. The Customs House at the other end of Queen Street at Petrie Bight was built a year later in a classic Revivalist style. It features twin pediments containing heraldic shields and the message 'Advance Australia'.

St Stephen's Church in Elizabeth Street is the oldest existing church in Brisbane. Completed in 1850, it provides one of the most striking contrasts between the old city and the new as it reflects in the gold AMP Tower and on the many changes to Brisbane. St John's Cathedral, Ann Street, was built in 1901. However, the Deanery in its grounds was built in 1853 by Queensland's first free settler, Andrew Petrie. The proclamation of the Colony of Queensland was read from the east balcony in 1859. Old Government House in George Street was the home of Queensland's first Governor and is today the appropriate headquarters of the National Trust of Queensland. Graceful old homes are also rich in history. Newstead House, the oldest home in the state, was built in 1846 at Newstead. Ormiston House at Ormiston was built in 1853. Other imposing residences include Palma Rosa, built in Albion in 1887, and Miegunyah in Jordan Terrace, Bowen Hills, built in 1894. Other links with the city's past can be viewed at the City Hall Art Gallery and Museum within the City Hall, the GPO Museum, the Queensland Museum at the Cultural Centre and in the museums at the University of Queensland.

FLOW WITH THE TIDE

1987 was Brisbane's Year of the River. It was a year to focus public attention on the river, its many uses and its potential as a place for recreation and enjoyment. The same public attention was directed towards Moreton Bay in 1989, the Year of the Bay. These promotional campaigns, which concentrated heavily on scientific and environmental aspects as well as recreation, helped to re-establish the historical links between Brisbane and its surrounding water environment. The Year of the River brought leisure boats to the river and saw the development of many public facilities along the riverbank. Parasailing and water skiing are now regular river activities, and the river acts as a spectacular backdrop to the Riverside Markets and the River Stage behind the City Botanic Gardens. The river is part of the character of the city and has played a major role in the growth of Brisbane. In the early days of settlement, paddle steamers and cargo boats brought supplies. In 1893, a major flood swept away the Victoria Bridge and made boats, not horse-drawn wagons, the mode of transport in Queen Street.

*Chinatown in Brisbane's Fortitude Valley has, like all good Chinatowns, its own 'lion' to bring good fortune. The lion dance adds a special touch to parades on celebrations such as the Chinese New Year in early February. The city's former long-serving Lord Mayor, Alderman Sallyanne Atkinson, makes friends (**below**).*

B risbane is a sprawling city. Its 1220 square kilometres makes it one of the 'largest' cities in the world, a fact that proud Brisbaneites regularly recall for incredulous visitors. (Moggill and Cape Moreton are 80 kilometres apart.) Today though, the boundary is a line on a map for the urban sprawl extends to the surrounding Ipswich, Logan and Redcliffe Cities and the Pine Rivers, Moreton and Redland Shires.

Brisbane is an historic accident from 1925 when a number of autonomous councils were amalgamated into a City of Brisbane scheme. For many years, residents had the benefits of regional planning and Brisbane City Council-run utilities including water supply, sewerage, transport and even electricity. Changes have reduced the extent of council responsibility but Brisbane remains regarded as a city-state, overseen by 26 aldermen representing local areas and a Lord Mayor who are elected and paid for full-time duties which can involve budgets exceeding $600 million. For a sprawling city, the central business district is an enigma as the panoramic aerial view (**top right**) shows. Most of the city's and indeed Queensland's commercial and government business can be done and hotel accommodation found within a 10-minute walk of the site of the 1825-42 convict settlement.

Four road bridges, a rail bridge, an expressway and three major roads take people to and from the CBD hub in a bend of the river, mostly enclosed by Albert and Victoria Parks and the sprawling Roma Street railway goods yard. Buildings from the Victorian era give an elegant if contrastingly quaint touch to the inner city where many 1900-1960 structures have been demolished for multi-storey and tower blocks, often glary in summer and throwing shadows in winter. People like to enjoy the delights of a few inner city parklands in sunshine (**right**). Use of public transport and pooling are becoming more common. Cars are left at home for night-time and weekend shopping at numerous expanded urban shopping complexes that have forced many former city-based stores to move or to close. For all that, the sight of central Brisbane is sufficient for some 800 000 residents to know that this is home.

BRISBANE CITY

Many a worker and visitor escapes from the hustle of central Brisbane with a walk along the paths of the old Botanic Gardens, including the one along the river (**above**). The Gardens, bounded by the river and George and Alice Streets, have been an admired part of Brisbane since convict days when the land was used for officers' gardens. Its 18 hectares were set aside officially in 1855, four years before Queensland's separation from New South Wales and declaration as a colony. This was a time of acclimatisation when many trees, plants and crops were brought from interstate and overseas by botanists and settlers to see whether they would thrive in the sub-tropical climate. Some of Queensland's first sugar cane was planted here as was possibly Queensland's first jacaranda tree, imported from Brazil. One hundred species of palms grow here and some trees such as Bunya pines planted more than a century ago survive. Few people enjoy the more open spaces of Albert Park, off Wickham Terrace (**right**). The Gardens and Albert Park have open air amphitheatres for stage and musical presentations.

In Australia, Brisbane has been regarded as a conservative, rather slow-changing city but that view is several decades out of date as the skyline indicates. There are now numerous occasions during the year when the city and its residents have an extra burst of life, as signified by fireworks exploding over the South Brisbane Reach of the Brisbane River with a sweeping arch of the Victoria bridge in the foreground (**bottom left**). Not strictly in the city but certainly overlooking a busy part of it is the Normanby Hotel (**below**). This establishment at the corner of Musgrave and Kelvin Grove Roads at the Normanby fiveways has helped slake the thirsts of many a traveller since 1891. Fresh paint shows the unique architecture of this building to advantage as well as drawing attention to its existence to seek custom. Long considered part of the Petrie Terrace precinct, the Normanby's economic future must be uncertain as the Hale Street extensions put the hotel in a no man's land triangle of traffic with no parking.

View down Albert Street (**above**) from the
landmark Suncorp Building is vastly different
from that of even 30 years ago. The City
Hall and tower now overlooks a King
George Square that is the landscaped and
paved roof of a multi-level underground
carpark instead of a narrow, car-jammed
Albert Street divided by a sandstone block
plinth bearing a bronze statue of King George
V mounted. The Reserve Bank building at
left, the Commonwealth Bank building at
right, and the T and G Building next on have
replaced old buildings, while Albert Street
has gone underground to service a bus
terminal. A band playing old time favourites is
a regular busking treat beneath the canopy
in the City Mall at what was the Queen and
Albert Streets corner (**right**).

Amid the new, the old are prominent. The Albert Street Uniting Church's red brick construction, slate roof and spire (**above left**) have long been a part of inner Brisbane's religious scene and subject of tourist cameras. Facade of the old Central Railway Station has been preserved in the station's redevelopment in association with the Sheraton Hotel (**left**). The old Executive Building between George and William Streets next to Queens Park (**top**) was where Queensland Cabinets met for much of this century. Queen Victoria's statute stands high above the park. Sculpture, fountain and flowerbeds replace what before 1968 was a busy tram stop at 'the smarter end of Queen Street' (**above**).

23

Old and the new of Brisbane are typified in the picture at **right** from the Brisbane River Town Reach. Moored at its Pier Nine base is Kookaburra Queen II, a replica stern paddlewheeler, built in timber in Brisbane in the 1980s as a companion paddlewheeler to Kookaburra Queen I. They are used for dining excursions and functions on the Brisbane River. Behind the new waterfrontage are multi-story buildings among a score of tower blocks built in this part of the inner city in the last 20 years including Waterfront Place (left). The same inner city area at dusk with the Story Bridge dominating the foreground as seen from New Farm (**below**).

A fiery trail and an eerie glow are left over the city and Story Bridge by a pass of an F-111 reconnaissance-bomber (**above**). Terrain-guidance radar enables Australia's most sophisticated military machine to approach downriver. On cue, the pilot does a 'fuel dump' and the fuel is set alight by the twin-jet exhausts. King George Square and the City Hall take on a new appearance on a stormy December night (**left**).

*Floodlit rugged cliffs of Kangaroo Point provide a different skyline feature over the Town Reach of the Brisbane River (**above**). As the festooned Story Bridge is prominent, so is the dark of the Botanic Gardens at left. The prominent double light is the weather beacon on the M.L.C. Building indicating fine, mild conditions — typical Brisbane.*

No other development in the inner Brisbane area had as great an effect on the community in the 1980s as the City Mall. What was the city's main street, Queen Street, was closed to traffic for two blocks between Edward and George Streets. The area was turned over to pedestrians who instantly appreciated being able to 'jay walk' Queen Street on brick pavements among landscaping, stages, sculptures and several open dining areas as they went about their business, shopping and leisure. Several canopy areas and seats invited visitors and locals to tarry awhile to watch the passing parade in some comfort, too. The Brisbane City Heart Business Association and the Brisbane City Council combined forces to plan and manage the City Mall, the cost of which is contributed to through a levy on businesses in the vicinity. After all, the Mall has helped stem the drift of trade and business to the suburbs so many here stand to benefit. Nineteenth century style steelwork supports a canopy to shade Mall visitors watching a presentation on the Top Stage (**below**). Trees help soften Mall constructions such as a first floor level walkway and shade seats for tired strollers (**right, top and bottom**).

Natural light floods through the clear roof section of the canopy now shading the central city Queen and Albert Streets corner of the City Mall (**left**). Open facade of the new Broadway arcade at the City Mall end (**below left**) entices shoppers to multi-levels of shops. Facade of the old Telegraph Newspaper building in Queen Street (**below**). This and the facades of several other old prominent Brisbane buildings adjacent like the Hotel Carlton have been retained on the Queen Street frontage of the huge Myer Centre.

Recently-restored St Stephen's Roman Catholic Cathedral fronting Elizabeth Street has an air of quiet elegance from another era when compared with the glass and concrete appearances of nearby tower blocks (**above right**). The cathedral's stained glass windows are more pleasing. Arguably, the Cathedral in its present position dating from 1874 has never been large enough for the Roman Catholic diocese. A Fortitude Valley site held ready for many years for a large cathedral was sold for commercial development. Everyone loves a parade, so it's said. Brisbane people are no exception and turn out in varying numbers to participate or watch depending on the subject and the weather. For more than 20 years, the procession associated with the city's Warana Festival in September-October has been the most colourful and attracted most participants and viewers. Almost without exception, the Festival has been held under blue skies, the meaning attributed to the Aboriginal word 'warana'. The closure of Queen Street for the City Mall caused the procession to be re-routed via Adelaide Street — to the delight of spectators on the steps of King George Square in front of the City Hall (**right**). The same clear blue skies in winter and spring in particular are reflected in the river about the city and give a view to Flinders Peak and far beyond to the Great Dividing Range (**opposite**).

Brisbaneites and visitors cannot complain about the lack of variety of landscape about the inner city as scenes on these pages prove. Pigeons are regular inhabitants of the Post Office Square (**above**), remaining well fed despite the regular attempts by Brisbane City Council cleaners to remove every crumb dropped by workers on lunchbreaks. Queen Street separates this first-floor level park from the General Post Office. The Botanic Gardens also has paved areas, used for performances by groups such as marching bands and for assembly and dispersal of city procession participants (**above right**). Regular cleaning and restoration schedules ensure the old Treasury Building (**opposite, top right**) is kept as one of the finest examples of Italianate buildings in the southern hemisphere. Debate about the building's future purpose continues. Roma Street forum area and adjacent Transport Department parklands (**opposite, top left**) are another large inner-city breathing space between King George Square and the Brisbane Transit Centre. The Brisbane Markets once occupied this site. The Brisbane River becomes a stretched rainbow in the time exposure photograph of the downtown business sector from Kangaroo Point (**right**). The Riverside complex is at right. The Pier Nine complex is the series of well-lit buildings in mid-picture.

Similar inner-city skyline by early morning light as seen by paddlers and ferry users passing Captain Burke Park, Kangaroo Point, under the Story Bridge (**above**). The only building in this picture not built in the last 30 years is the Australian Customs House at the bottom end of Queen Street at right, distinguished by its columns and copper-domed roof, not always appreciated by Queen Street pedestrians. Remains of the Patrick's and Circular Quay wharf areas, once hub of Brisbane's thriving city port more than three-quarters of a century ago, are destined to be replaced with more riverside walkways associated with office blocks. Atrium of the new Myer Centre, bounded by Elizabeth, Albert and Queen Streets, as seen from a ground floor dining area (**right**). This development, bearing the name of the department store chain, has brought many changes to shops and shopping in the inner city. Included was an underground bus terminus, and retention of the facades of several old prominent buildings including the Telegraph Newspaper and Hotel Carlton.

Landscaping has become essential feature to soften the otherwise 'hard' surrounds of new city buildings, despite the worth of the land (**top**).

The Breakfast Creek Hotel, by the creek named by explorer John Oxley, (**above right**) is popular for its beer served from wooden barrels and for its barbecue steaks. Newstead House (**above left**) on the other side of Breakfast Creek is the city's oldest residential building dating from 1846. Many of its rooms have been restored and furnished in 19th century style.

Different aspect of central Brisbane, this time as seen from the Performing Arts Complex, South Brisbane (*right*). Dominating the river area are the South-east Freeway off the Captain Cook Bridge at right and the Victoria Bridge at left. While all buildings appear to be modern, this scene includes one of Brisbane's oldest buildings, the basement of the old Stores building, dating from 1829, floodlit at lower right. Fully lit at right is the Queensland Government's Executive Building. At mid-picture is the MLC Building, known for its rooftop weather beacon. The sweeping Victoria Bridge is the third such structure across the river about this point. Old Government House, George Street, (*below*) was built in 1860-62 for Queensland's first Governor, Sir George Ferguson Bowen. It was the official residence of succeeding Governors until the present Government House at Bardon was completed in 1910. This restored building is occupied by the National Trust of Queensland.

*Alice Street entrance to the Queensland Club (**left**), diagonally opposite Parliament House. This fine building housing a gentlemen's club and accommodation also dates from the 19th century. Roseville, another old Brisbane residence at Newstead (**above**), now restored and operated as a fine restaurant.*

Brisbane and Queensland have long had communities of Chinese people. Many families can trace their lineage many generations back to those who came from China, Hong Kong, Singapore and the United States to try their luck in the new goldfields of the colony in its first 30 years. They remained to become part of the business scene, often running enterprises associated with food such as market gardens and restaurants. The Joss House in Higgs Street, Breakfast Creek, is a Buddhist temple built in 1884 for the Chinese market gardeners of the area by workmen with materials brought from China (**top right**). After 1930, the building fell into decay. In 1966, the Chinese community helped restore the Joss House and it is now maintained and used particularly by elderly Chinese. The Brisbane City Council and Chinese businessmen have helped establish a Chinatown in the Valley area. Distinctive buildings, gardens and signs in English and Chinese characters have given a new appearance to the Chinatown Mall in Duncan Street (**opposite, top**). Firecrackers explode during a lion dance in the Mall to ward off evil spirits and to bring good fortune to all, part of Chinese New Year festivities in Brisbane's Chinatown (**right**).

New atrium-style interior of the McWhirter's building in Brisbane's Fortitude Valley (**left**). McWhirter's was a large department store for many years before its takeover by the Myer group. The store was closed down until the building was bought and refurbished recently in a major attempt to return shoppers to the Valley area. The ground floor is large food hall. Other floors feature speciality shops and an area for artists to display their arts and crafts.

Large ponds and palm trees are a feature of the City Botanic Gardens (**above**). They contain fish and have attracted a wide range of water creatures and waterfowl which remain because of food proferred by visitors. Azalea bush in full flower in the Botanic Gardens (**right**). This is a prominent species in many private gardens growing in profusion in Brisbane's climate and providing great splashes of pink and white. The Botanic Gardens is also used for many attractions during the year, and is often dotted with stalls on occasions such as the Warana Festival and Australia Day (**opposite top**). Education without tears provided you are careful! School children are given a guided tour of the Botanic Gardens succulents section to be told why some have sharp points (**opposite left**). Volunteer guides impart some of the knowledge during pre-arranged conducted tours of the Botanic Gardens (**opposite right**).

South transcept of St John's Anglican Cathedral, Ann Street, Brisbane (**above**). Extensions under way to the west front of this fine stone building may mean that this building may be the first Gothic cathedral to be completed in the 21st century! Such construction demands modern methods and engineering but also skilled stone masons.

Nineteenth century style of Naldham House (**left**) is retained by the Brisbane Polo Club, a new inner-city club for business and professional people. This building at 1 Eagle Street may soon be the only extant structure giving a reminder of the past when many shipping companies operated from this part of the city. Queensland Parliament House, George Street, as seen from the Botanic Gardens gate (**bottom left**). In the background is the multi-storey Parliamentary Annexe which houses parliamentary offices, facilities including the Parliamentary Library, and accommodation for Ministers and out-of-town Members. Queensland's Colonial Architect Charles Tiffin won a 200 guinea ($420) prize for his design of this Renaissance-style building. The foundation stone was laid in 1865 and, except for short periods for refurbishment, the House has been in continuous use. Its stone was quarried at Goodna and its red cedar hewn in the Canungra district. Only in recent years has the stone portico section been added. Because Queensland has had only a Legislative Assembly house since 1922, the Legislative Council chamber in the building is used only on ceremonial occasions. The Mansions is another Queensland Government building in George Street (**below**) restored to its 1889 style and occupied by businesses associated with built heritage.

Aerial view over the city as seen by very few people (**above**). This airspace is under the command of busy Brisbane Airport air traffic controllers. It looks north-east along the Town Reach. At left are the Queensland University of Technology and Queensland Parliament Buildings and the City Botanic Gardens. At right at the Kangaroo Point cliffs and River Terrace leading to the Story Bridge in mid-distance.

Sunlight reflects off the Central Plaza One and Two tower blocks in downtown Brisbane (**opposite top left**). Their Japanese architect took crystal shapes as his model. Swivelling rooftop mounted gantries catch many a passerby unawares. These are used by window cleaners on a never-ending job.

Ornate Mooney fountain at the corner of Queen and Eagle Streets with the Riverside tower in the background (**above**). This 19th century memorial is to a fireman who died while fighting a blaze in this area. People turn out in force in the Mall for special occasions (**left**), usually for sporting heroes or teams to make a triumphant return to their home city.

*Outboard-powered speedboat scarcely leaves a wake as its sleek hull planes over the Brisbane River during a competition event (**below**). Such haste belies the tranquil nature of the river as it meanders through its lower reaches — a character long reflected in the lifestyle of residents of Queensland's capital city.*

Who would have thought that less than two centuries have passed since the river's discovery and traverse by New South Wales Surveyor-General John Oxley in a whaleboat? Shipwreck survivor John Finnegan directed the 1823 discovery for he had crossed the river mouth bar (only about 1.5 metres at low water) in his quest for civilisation. For two days, Oxley's crew off H.M. cutter Mermaid must have toiled and sweated under the December sun as they rowed some 60 kilometres up-river as far as an area now known as Prior's Pocket, opposite Goodna. On his return to the mouth, he gave the name of Brisbane to the river in honour of the then Governor of New South Wales, Sir Thomas Brisbane.

In this and subsequent voyages, Oxley recorded the river in its undisturbed state noting sand, shingle and shoals and the tropical nature of the fringing vegetation including Bribie Island and hoop pines, crow's ash, blue gum and brown applegum. Such scenery was 'particularly beautiful'. Surprisingly, most plant species mentioned by the early explorers can still be seen along its banks but native species now occur as regrowth or remnants rather than part of distinct communities. Riverine forest behind Dewar Terrace, Corinda, today retains much of its natural appearance, a view taken for granted by water skiers from Mandalay opposite (**right**).

From time to time, large volume floods such as that of 1974 and farmland and urban runoff have and will continue to muddy the river and its tributaries, large and small. But environment-conscious Brisbaneites in the 1990s need not apologise for the state of their river. Basically, it's clean. Its just since 1862, dredging for navigation, flood mitigation work and construction materials has increased the river's diurnal tidal 'salt wedge' upstream. Fine silts are held in suspension for longer thus the Brisbane River appears more 'turbid' than many, particularly during flood tides of more than two metres in the city reaches. Mangroves have extended their local range upstream!

The river and its tributaries have been good to Brisbane and to Queensland providing its water supply, a transport link, and the state's major commercial shipping resource. In recent years, the community and its leaders have given new respect to the dear old Brisbane River. In future, we can expect fewer phantom waste discharges and stiff penalties for those who pollute via buried pipes. We can't expect a crystal clean stream but we can enjoy the river via cruises, ferries, and pleasure boats and by car through landscaped gardens along its banks. The bicycle way-cum-footpath between Toowong and Parliament House provides an idyllic respite between the meandering river and two of Brisbane's busiest thoroughfares — Coronation Drive and North Quay (**right**).

THE RIVER

Many a yachtie cruising the Australian coast or circumnavigating the world remembers Brisbane from the Town Reach (**above**). Here, large piles have given safe river moorings to all shapes and sizes of craft, particularly in the December-April 'cyclone season' along the Queensland coast. Crews enjoy a break from coastal scenery, often earning useful dollars in casual work to refurbish their craft and replenish larders to see them through the next leg or so of their journey. For a small fee, they share the outlook of the river, Story Bridge, and Kangaroo Point with the occupiers of some of Brisbane's prime commercial office space as well as Parliament House and the Queensland University of Technology. They paddle tiny dinghies to nearby ferry pontoons for a five-minute walk to downtown Brisbane for their supplies or for brief stints as land-lubbers strolling through the adjacent City Botanic Gardens.

Drum moorings stem to stern are simpler to use for non-resident yachties such as this haven at Corinda (**left**). Despite its length, the Brisbane River's currents prevent the location of many, safe, permanent moorings in its curving reaches, particularly upstream of the city. Also, the cruising waters of Moreton Bay are many hours away from these moorings. This is okay with a following breeze and a good ebb tide under the keel but the return in opposite conditions can make the river trip a very long voyage at the end of a short weekend on the Bay. Yet to venture upstream can be a most pleasant experience. These days, Seventeen Mile Rocks pose little hazard and even large launches can reach the junction with the Bremer River at Brisbane's official boundary. Sunset over the adjacent Moggill Reach can be a reflective experience (**below**). Many a time there's no suggestion of conditions depicted by wavy blue lines in Brisbane's coat of arms.

The Brisbane River takes on a multi-coloured appearance at night when on special occasions more than usual office lights are left on and intense illuminations of buildings are reflected from the surface as seen from Moray Street, New Farm (**above**). This is a new dimension, particularly of downtown Brisbane where glass and concrete multi-storey tower blocks have changed the patterns of the city's business life and that of its inhabitants, particularly in the last decade. This is the area along the streets with the names of English queens — Mary, Margaret and Alice Streets, one king (Edward), and outsiders Eagle, Felix and Market Streets. The festooned Story Bridge linking Kangaroo Point on the southside with Fortitude Valley on the north remains prominent on the city skyline as it has done since the 1930s. 'I'd rather be sailing' is a popular bumper sticker message. Chances are that many a Monday to Friday business person in these offices takes the advice and breathes fresh rather than dried, filtered and chilled air on Saturday and Sunday. Double-ended yacht (**right**) bears the symbol of the Royal Queensland Yacht Squadron, headquartered for many years near the city but now operating out of the built harbour at Manly on Moreton Bay.

Meanderings of the Brisbane River in its downstream reaches are readily apparent in two forms. A street directory confirms that close suburbs across the river from one another are a long way around via the bridges. Dutton Park is but three kilometres from Mowbray Park as the crow flies but 12 kilometres via the river, the route often taken by fruit bats at dusk for several months of the year as they fly from upstream 'camps' such as at Indooroopilly Island to foray backyard crops. The second depends on air traffic controllers at Brisbane Airport. Still early mornings have been found ideal for a 'drift' over the central city in hot air balloons. Intrepid adventurers looking south-west from over New Farm have the vista *(above)*. At right is Fortitude Valley with the central business district in mid-picture. At left is the green of the City Botanic Gardens with the white Captain Cook Bridge of the city's South-east Freeway. In the foreground, the finger of Kangaroo Point supports the Bradfield Highway approach to the Story Bridge and splits the Town and Shafston Reaches. Competitive sailing on the river *(left)* has its wind and direction limits. In summer, clubs at Bulimba, West End and Chelmer hold regular races for classes from junior two-up sabots to 18-footers at world championship standard.

Parklands fringe many parts of the river giving a green, shaded outlook for their visitors. Orleigh Park, West End, (**right**) has views over the Toowong and St Lucia reaches towards some of Brisbane's most stately homes and units. Further upstream at the Sherwood Reach (**below**), past floods have ensured that homes have been sited well back from its banks. Carrington Rocks give protection to a small boat mooring area here. The river and the Story Bridge have been found to be ideal for fireworks extravaganzas (**bottom left**) as spectators on both banks have uninterrupted views. St Lucia ferry terminal (**bottom right**) is used by residents commuting to the southside, and by University of Queensland students taking the reverse journey.

Riverfront property is highly sought after and the river's length provides many sites and aspects (*left*). While residents enjoy the outlook and cooling breezes said to blow off the river, few venture on the water. A fast spin in a launch can be fun at high tide but the skipper's lot may be at low ebb when forced ashore through the mud later on the bottom of the tide. Small jetties and pontoons give owners exclusive use of their section of the river for line fishing and crabbing using wire or cane 'pots' and net 'dillies'.

Development of Jindalee and adjacent suburbs in the 1960s and '70s brought large-scale urban planning to Brisbane. This provided for a variety of serviced homesites off sealed and kerbed streets. Another benefit was provision for long strips of parkland along the river (*above*).

Massive span of the Gateway Bridge between Eagle Farm and Murarrie as seen from river level (**right**).This 1980s landmark is a vital link for traffic bypassing the central city. Congestion in a more sedate fashion (**above**) as launches anchor opposite Toowong's Regatta Hotel at jacaranda blooming time.

River-based lifestyle is what you make it year-round in Brisbane's climate. Wind twisting around St Lucia unit blocks brings spinnaker problems to South Brisbane Sailing Club members near their West End base (**top**). Walkways projecting over the river banks at the Riverside Centre (**above**) and Pier Nine have brought a new outlook for diners, strollers and ferry travellers in the city. At the Carrington Boat Club, Corinda (**top left**), jetties from the banks provide safe moorings for small yachts and launches nose-in fashion as well as convenient stands for those attracted to line fishing.

Yachts, a launch and a houseboat lie ready at Corinda (**far left**) to take their owners out on the water. Many live in suburbs only a few minutes' drive away so necessary maintenance is less of a task than at more distant moorings. Swimming, fishing and canoeing are enjoyed by local children on quiet waters off Kinellan Point, Merthyr Park, New Farm (**left**). One of the world's famous ships, Queen Elizabeth II, (**below left** at the Fisherman Islands container terminal at the river mouth) provides water-based recreation of a different dimension for its patrons.

New Brisbane City Council Cityferry services such as at the Riverside pontoon (**top**) provide rapid transport without the chance of a traffic jam. The Brisbane-built Kookaburra Queen paddlewheeler (**above**) replicates the past in a modern style to offer river cruises and dining.

*High-pitched galvanised iron roof tops a typical old Queensland-style house (**below**). Such a house typifies a past era when workers' residences were relatively close to central Brisbane industry and commerce. Some residents remain here (**below right**). Darling Point, Wynnum, Manly and Lota overlooking Moreton Bay (**right**) are desirable suburban addresses.*

Any city does not comprise merely of a central business district, public buildings, and other places of work. It survives only because of a much larger surrounding area from which it draws wealth and where its people can live and play. As explained earlier, Brisbane's extent is much greater than could be expected for a metropolitan area of its population. Consequently, it can lay claim to a long list of localities which together are considered as 'the suburbs'. Except with recent planned developments, these have tended to grow along the main transport routes in and out of Brisbane. Ipswich Road, Logan Road, Beaudesert Road, Old Cleveland Road, Sandgate Road, Gympie Road and Samford Road are reminders of the links between Brisbane and other places established more than a century ago. Their tortuous natures are said to reflect the easiest routes taken by goods wagons drawn by teams of bullocks. Similarly, railways followed more level routes avoiding cuttings, tunnels and bridges where possible. Brisbane's electric tramway system, in operation to 1968, had similar constraints. Construction was not always easy and the term 'Brisbane — city of seven hills' was an apt description used until recent years.

In typical Australian manner, Brisbane residents sought their own blocks of land on which to live. Terraced houses along narrow streets were not for them when there was plenty of land. Quaintly, Queensland adopted an old English style of land measurement based on 100 links making up a surveyor's chain of the imperial length of 66 feet. Land was measured in 'perches', a perch covering 30 and a quarter square feet. Typical housing blocks were 16, 24 or 32 perches — terms on titles and appearing in advertisements still today rather than 404, 607 and 809 square metres. To have a 32 perch block in a leafy quiet suburb of Brisbane was proof indeed a person had succeeded in business or a profession because an appropriately sized mansion could then be built on it.

Even two generations ago before World War II, plenty of land was available for housing within 10 kilometres of the city centre. Like all cities, prime positions on hilltops with broad aspects or in secluded areas considered 'up market' were long taken. Land values today continue to reflect the merit of suburbs such as Hamilton, Ascot and Clayfield, Toowong and Indooroopilly. Suburban names reflect a curious mixture of old world places, people, and corruptions or contractions of what early settlers believed they heard from local Aborigines. Names like Annerley, Ashgrove, Holland Park, St John's Wood, Highgate Hill, Sherwood, and Paddington have obvious connections with Britain. The names Lutwyche, Chermside, MacGregor, Petrie and Leichhardt in titles reflect Brisbane's early history. Unique to Brisbane are the tongue-twisting Woolloongabba, Coorparoo, Murarrie, Indooroopilly, Yeronga, Yeerongpilly, Kurilpa, Bulimba, Jindalee and Wooloowin. Names such as Jamboree Heights, Westlake, Riverhills, Karana Downs and Bridgeman Downs have been adopted since 1960. A Brisbane strategic plan proposes more dense living in and around 15 urban nodes.

THE SUBURBS

In the past, land developers might have been blamed entirely for offering urban land bulldozed clear of vegetation and topsoil. Modern-day buyers demand blocks with natural vegetation and minimum disturbance for services. In the last two decades, the city has taken a 'green' direction as the picture (**right**) graphically portrays. Trees, shrubs and grasslands dominate this wide angle aerial view from Kenmore over the south-western suburbs towards the city. At left is the Western Freeway below Mt Coot-tha. In mid-picture is Indooroopilly with road and rail bridges crossing the river. At right are the suburbs of Chelmer and Graceville. Several characteristics can help identify old and often restored Queensland-style houses. Almost always, they are high set on stumps to cool the underneath (these days partly bricked or blocked in), have covered verandahs to help shade the inner house, and have some form of decoration around the verandah, partly to stop young children falling off! Fine castings (or their aluminium copies) are shown to great effect on houses (**below**, and **below right**). They are less obvious in others (**opposite bottom left**). Other owners make use of plentiful supplies of timber to create patterns in railings (**opposite bottom right**).

Not all 'old Queenslander' style buildings are old. Present day architects have cause to use the style when designing buildings to fit comfortably alongside existing buildings such as those in the Paddington precinct. The speciality offices and shops building (**right**) has a high roof of galvanised iron with ventilators, awnings of curved iron, and guttering and downpiping to match. (The curved iron reflects the once frequent use of a rolling machine to make panels for galvanised iron water tanks.) It is set in landscaped grounds with a paved parking area. Unfortunately, not all property developers go to such trouble when planning more modern urban shopping buildings.

New Farm Park is noted for its roses and its avenues of jacaranda trees which bloom in profusion in October (**above**). Jacaranda flowers create a mauve carpet for park strollers (**right**). Narrow beachfront of the Bayside suburb of Manly takes on a new appearance as the best place from which to conduct sailboarding marathons (**opposite top**). Australian Woolshed attraction at Ferny Grove means a visitor to Australia needs travel no more than 12 kilometres from the central city to see a typical woolshed, complete with eager sheepdog (**opposite left**). Brisbane's warmer months — September to March — find many a youngster seeking to cool off in a pool. Several suburbs have waterslides to add to the fun (**opposite right**).

Main buildings of the University of Queensland in the suburb of St Lucia are faced with Helidon freestone, a form of sandstone, and feature friezes and shield decorations (*right*). The new Brisbane Airport, sometimes host to international flying troupes (*below*), was built on sand pumped from Moreton Bay. Canal estates in some near-Brisbane areas have been created by pumping out channels and using sand and mud to build levels for waterfront housing (*bottom*).

The new Brisbane Airport is only a 15-minute drive from the central city, an achievement for planners seeking to balance the needs of a suitable, convenient spot and minimising noise nuisance along flight paths. A central arrival/departures building with covered walkway 'fingers' and extensive short and long-term car parking (**left**) is a far cry from the former Eagle Farm complex which grew out of a grassy paddock in the 1930s and a World War II airbase. The air traffic control tower has given Brisbane a new landmark. Planners for Centenary Estates developers in the 1960s made provision for recreation in what was then an outlying urban area. The result today is the fine McLeod Country Golf Course at Mt Ommaney (**below**). This and the Jindalee Golf Course provide green landscapes and fine sporting venues for residents of the surrounding suburbs of Jindalee, Jamboree Heights, Middle Park, Westlake and Riverhills. The developer also provided the Centenary Bridge over the Brisbane River and part of the Centenary Highway, now a fast, major southwestern outlet for Brisbane.

The Garden City Shopping Complex at Upper Mt Gravatt (**above**) was one of Brisbane's first major suburban shopping complexes in the 1960s and has been steadily expanding as pressures of population growth along the Brisbane south-east corridor increased. Similar complexes at Indooroopilly, Mitchelton, Chermside, Aspley, Toombul, Cannon Hill and Sunnybank have changed the shopping patterns of Brisbane residents in the last two decades. Many of the former local corner stores have been forced to close. Business can often be completed in the suburbs without having to go into the city. Further urban shopping complexes are proposed, the largest being at Boondall. The Brisbane City Council has had to juggle with demands to retain the wetlands conservation values of the extensive flats around Cabbage Tree Creek with pressures to develop. Without great care, precious opportunities of say fishing in the creek mouth (**right**) could be limited and possibly lost to future generations.

For many years, the lack of suitable venues limited Brisbane's participation in major sporting and other events. Construction of the Queen Elizabeth II Jubilee Sporting Centre at Nathan (**left**) in the 1970s introduced a new era. A direct outcome was Brisbane's staging of the 1982 Commonwealth Games. Such an investment is not required for sailing for Moreton Bay waters are most suitable for events including those held over Olympic courses. Sandy foreshores of Wellington Point are often a great starting point for a day's sailing in laser and catamaran classes (**below**). Dawn breaks over Manly boat harbour (**bottom**), now the permanent haven for more than 1000 yachts and motor cruisers spread over four marina complexes.

*Flock of shags in laboured flight **(below)** winging their way to another fishing area along the shores of Moreton Bay. They are often observed at rest in a half-flight pose, seemingly grounded while waiting for their wings to dry. From this comes the expression 'shag on a rock' meaning 'left without support'.*

*Early morning coastal view looking north from Maroochydore on the Sunshine Coast **(top right)** is an impressive scene setter. Coastal banksias **(bottom right)** add a golden touch to places like Stradbroke Island.*

Few cities would be as fortunate as Brisbane for having such variety of scenery and attractions within 150 kilometres or a couple of hours drive of the city. In fact, many are so close some people choose to live at these places and commute to the city by fast electric train, ferry, bus or car daily. At weekends and holidays, traffic is never heavy enough to deter Brisbaneites from venturing in all directions for even a day visit.

East of the city lies Moreton Bay with its main fringing islands of Bribie, Moreton, and North and South Stradbroke. Within the Bay lie St Helena, Mud, Green and Peel Islands, the inhabited Macleay, Lamb, Karragarra and Russell Islands, and numerous mangrove-fringed islands of sand and mud. (The Bay is also the estuary of the major river systems of the Brisbane, Pine, Logan, Coomera and Nerang.) To the south lies the Gold Coast, a 30-kilometre long stretch of sandy beach, backed by development so extensive that it has long grown into a city in its own right. At any time, its population is made up of retirees, workers and tourists. Its mountain-backed hinterland is aptly described as the 'green behind the gold'. To the north, there is the equally famous and, some may say, more attractive area of the Sunshine Coast. This is another long strip of beaches from Caloundra to Noosa Heads, backed largely by residential development. Its green backdrop is Buderim Mountain, the Maroochy Valley, Nambour, and the Blackall Range. One may also venture to Brisbane's west through the Bremer and Lockyer Valleys to the Great Dividing Range and the inland cities of Toowoomba and Warwick. Not named but equally important and dynamic are scores of communities and locations in between. In this south-east or Moreton Region live half of Queensland's population. For many reasons, this is one of the fastest growing areas of Australia with tens of thousands of people recorded as moving from interstate each year. Such movement puts great strains on authorities to cope with the present, much less plan for the future. While there are jobs to go to, water to drink, food to eat and houses to live in, much of the rest is free! It's hard not to refer to the climate. Days over 25 degrees deserve a day at a pool or at the beach. Mornings below 10 degrees deserve extra time in bed before clear sunshine warms the air and gives promise of a great day. On a world scale, rain is hardly ever cold. More than 25 millimetres often comes in a storm to refresh the latter part of the day. Provided then you carry a sweater in winter and have an umbrella handy in summer, you're set to enjoy Brisbane's surrounds.

SURROUNDS

When one comes down to basics, the Gold Coast would not be what it is without the beachfront. While on some days waves whipped to a frenzy by south-east gales pound the shore and erode the dunes, most times there's only roller after roller expending energy breaking and washing onto beaches of fine, off-white sand. Often tide marks are the only evidence of change. So many people enjoy the beach and particularly the surf that year-round arrangements have to be made to ensure swimmer safety. Surf lifesaving carnivals featuring belt and line contests (**right**) ensure weekend volunteer lifesavers are at peak efficiency for their difficult task. Development has been so constant on the Gold Coast since the 1950s that any aerial view is out of date shortly after it is taken. Be assured then that the view (**below**) is recent. Races for boats designed and built for rowing out through the waves for a possible rescue (**opposite left**) are another test of lifesaving proficiency. In less crowded areas, pied oyster-catchers, also known as redbills, comb the waterfront for telltale signs of shellfish which they manage to retrieve and open for a feed (**opposite right**).

The sea has always been a challenge. Humans have sought to exploit its resources and tame its awesome power. The Pacific Ocean off the Gold Coast has seen a variety of craft. Fisherman used oar-powered clinker boats. These were followed by inboard and outboard powered craft from inflatable 'rubber duckys' to sleek cruisers. Sail has been used by yachts, sport catamarans and aerobatic windsurfers. The waves have powered other devices dubbed surfboards, surfskis and kayaks. Oh for the thrill of 'catching' a wave on a board and 'riding' it to the shore (**right**). Snub-sterned modern lifesaver surfboat is a fine development of the fishermen's original (**opposite top**). The alternative between waves is simply to lie on the beach, like Surfers Paradise (**far top**) or stroll in adjacent beachfront shopping areas (**far bottom**). Coolangatta Beach (**below**) has been restored by pumping sand from offshore reserves.

Surfers Paradise beach, once the paradise for surfers in the day and for fishermen at night, is now rarely deserted. Early morning brings people scurrying like so many rabbits from their high rise 'burrows' to the fresh sea air and mist of the beachfront (**above**). Young couples hand in hand join retirees, swimmers, joggers, walkers and fitness freaks for strolls along the ever-changing sands. Skill of a surfboat crew of four oarsmen and a steering 'sweep' lies in picking lulls between the main waves to ensure a good start out through the breakers (**right**). The alternative is wasted energy and a swamped boat.

The Australian pelican, the local species of a family found in many countries, is a common inhabitant of sheltered coastal waters of southern Queensland *(top left)*. Its large body may appear ungainly but once airborne, the pelican is a master of powered flight, often soaring thousands of feet into the air to catch wind currents to and from inland breeding grounds. Its pouched bill is for holding fish before they are swallowed. Locals will tell you all pelicans disappear when they know suitable breeding conditions occur in inland Australia but there are always strays around the Gold Coast Broadwater, Moreton Bay, Pumicestone Passage, and the Maroochy and Noosa Rivers. Surf lifesaving carnivals are not all action. Like beach patrols, they involve many hours of patient waiting on the beach *(above and left)* while heats and other events are held before tightly-contested finals.

Lamington National Park is a 20 500 hectare natural reserve of sub-tropical rainforest, open forest and montane heathland along the McPherson Range south of Brisbane. Its lookouts provide panoramic views in all directions (**top left**) for its peaks reach almost 1200 metres. With Springbrook, Tamborine, Mt Chinghee, Mt Barney and Main Range National Parks, Lamington is part of a 'scenic rim' of reserves in a semicircle west and south of Brisbane. Many thousands of people visit these parks each year. While much of Lamington is inaccessible to all but keen bushwalkers, the Queensland National Parks and Wildlife Service maintains graded walking tracks from the Binna Burra and O'Reilly's resorts. Many tracks follow creek headwaters and pass innumerable waterfalls like the one **(opposite)**. The park abounds in wildlife though this is often hard to see in the daytime except where birds such as king parrots and crimson rosellas come to clearings to be fed seed (**above left**). The sugar glider (**above**) and the boobook owl (**bottom left**) are common nocturnal creatures.

To many Brisbane residents and visitors, the Sunshine Coast of today retains many of the less sophisticated, more natural charms once the preserve of the Gold Coast. They turn north for their relaxation and enjoyment. While the area has been settled for many years, Sunshine Coast local authorities have imposed strict planning guidelines to avoid what are seen as the basic mistakes of the Gold Coast like high rises casting afternoon shadows across the beaches. The improved Bruce Highway out of Brisbane and the Sunshine Coast motorway have reduced travelling times markedly making day visits to places as far as Noosa Heads an outing, not an ordeal. The beaches deserve rave notice in their own right. Substantial areas for esplanades, parks, recreation and nature conservation maintain a green look, particularly at Bribie Island, Currimundi, Mt Coolum, Peregian and Noosa. The view from Caloundra Head looking south-west over Kings Beach and Golden Beach with the Glasshouse Mountains in the background (**above**) typifies the Sunshine Coast's mix of built and natural environments.

Golden light over Pumicestone Passage finds pelicans waiting for fish — fresh from the water or skeletons by courtesy of lucky fishermen returning from 'wetting a line' (**below**). The Passage is a marine park where habitats are protected to help ensure fish stocks are maintained. Kings Beach, Caloundra (**bottom**) is always a popular surfing beach but conditions are ideal when in summer north-easterly and northerly winds blow instead of the prevailing south-easterlies. Canvas umbrellas provide essential shade when the midday sun's rays are fierce and sunbathers are urged to slip into a shirt, slop protective sunscreen lotion on all exposed skin and slap on a broad-brimmed sun hat, to lessen the risk of skin cancer.

Pumicestone Passage has not changed markedly since its name was bestowed in the 19th century after the discovery of the volcanic product along its shores. 'Rubbish. Wrong' some Brisbaneites and locals might say. How is it then that authorities have been able to make a marine park declaration over its tidal waters and a national park declaration along most of its Bribie Island frontage in the last decade and make the promise of more reserve? These actions will ensure the Passage remains as we first knew it — a mangrove-lined shallow area with constantly changing tortuous channels which can hardly be said to provide a 'passage' to boats much larger than dinghies and runabouts. The Bribie Island bridge between Ningi and Bongaree blocks many Bay-going craft from even attempting to run aground somewhere in the Passage, and entrance harbour proposals have been rejected. In the foreseeable future, the scene of pelicans being fed at a small boat anchorage (**below**) will be unchanged. The dramatic shape of Coonowrin in the sunset (**right**) is a reminder of the 1770 sighting and naming of this and adjacent peaks by Captain James Cook sailing well off the coast. Mt Crookneck (as it is now known) along with Mt Beerwah, Mt Tibrogargan and others are trachyte plugs, the remains of volcanic activity long past. Their scientific, historic and scenic interest have ensured the major peaks are within national parks. All may be climbed with care, and more than a little expertise in some parts. The Big Pineapple (**below right**) has become an artificial landmark on the southern approaches to Nambour. It draws many thousands of visitors a year to its surrounding showplace farming venture based on the district's outstanding quality pineapple production.

Estuary of the Mooloolah River at Mooloolaba has become one of Queensland's major small craft harbours by necessity. A sand bar at the Point Cartwright entrance to the sea was always a hazard for boat owners. But outside of an even shallower entrance at the Noosa River, there was no other shelter between Moreton Bay and the Wide Bay bar. The Queensland Government decision to end the use of ships for the Port of Brisbane pilot service off Caloundra brought a major change to Mooloolaba. Carefully designed entrance walls had to be built so replacement smaller vessels could use the river as a base in all but cyclonic weather. The result has been several major marinas and pile moorings for local and visiting vessels, and development of a major fishing port, yacht club and rescue service. When the ocean is only 10 minutes fast sailing away, yachting has become a major pastime along the Sunshine Coast. The Mooloolaba Yacht Club is a major supporter of sailing for juniors staging events and providing expertise for the next generation of its members (**top left**). The Yandina district north of Nambour has long been regarded as a prime farming area, particularly for crops of sugar cane which are sent to the Nambour mill for crushing. This fine colonial house adjacent to the Bruce Highway at Yandina (**left**) is indicative of the district's richness. Sugar cane grows in profusion along the Maroochy River flats under the Yandina's district landmark of Mt Ninderry (**below**).

Terrace house style of shops and offices at Montville on the crest of the Blackall Range, south-west of Nambour (**right**). In the last 20 years, the range strip from Maleny in the south to Mapleton in the north has become a prime centre for the creation, exhibition and sale of a wide range of arts and crafts. Artists in many fields have chosen to come here for a quiet lifestyle displacing many dairy farmers, at least along the range which offers fine views east over the Sunshine Coast and its hinterland. Roadside signs invite visitors to browse among a wide range of goods from paintings and pottery to leather goods and metal work. While sales are often made at homes and some galleries, there is also an outlet at craft markets held regularly at Range and nearby locations. Production of fine glassware demands special skills. The output of local artisans deserves admiration (**opposite**).

Primary production remains the mainstay of the economic progress of the Sunshine Coast hinterland. The growing of fruit and vegetables, ginger, nuts, and sugar cane along with dairying and timber getting are the prime activities. The world enjoys macadamia (or Queensland) nuts because of a tree found naturally in this area. Yandina is a leading producer of ginger and ginger products with major overseas export markets. Because of its extent, the growing of sugar cane is the most evident of these industries. Spectacular fires in late afternoons (**opposite bottom**) rid crops of 'trash', unwanted vegetable matter around the stalks, and vermin before mechanical harvesters move in. A farmer uses a drip fuel line (**below left**) to set the fire which he hopes will be a quick one. This time-honoured practice in the industry helped when cane was harvested by men using machetes but is being phased out because of its detrimental effect on the sugar content and because it pollutes the air. Pineapple farming requires not only good soil, often deep red loams, but special techniques to bring on the crop and avoid erosion. A farmer uses a tractor to rip a hillside in preparation for ploughing and planting (**below**). Cheap imports threaten the viability of Queensland pineapple growing.

A quaint crooked building with an old vehicle on the roof (**right**) is turning heads of drivers and passengers along the Bruce Highway at Palmview. The Ettamogah Pub is a real hotel based on the one in a long-running cartoon in Australasian Post magazine. Seagulls wait to scrounge scraps, a common beachfront sight (**below**). Centenary procession passing through central Nambour (**below right**). Remains of a shipwreck, still washed by waves at Caloundra (**bottom**).

Water is a force for good and evil and the effects of both are seen in Brisbane's surrounds. The Caloundra Bar end of the Pumicestone Passage as seen from Golden Beach, Caloundra *(above)*, appears a placid, stable waterway on a day of perfect weather. But really it is a dynamic coastal feature as indicated by the dune edges and dead trees. The trees once had a mud environment and thrived because they were adapted to it. Change has brought sand which has killed the trees but provided the base for beach spinifex grass to get a hold. Multiply this process a million times and you have some idea of why the Queensland coastline is changing constantly. Even without projected 'greenhouse effect' sea level rises, authorities can be hard pressed to determine outcomes vital to planning and construction. The Queensland Hydraulics Laboratory of the Queensland Department of Environment and Heritage at Deagon, Brisbane, is a unique facility where at least some parameters of the coastal processes can be reproduced in model form and the results observed. Engineers can predict outcomes with some certainty before costly civil engineering projects are undertaken. Wave action is a natural occurrence little understood by the community. The Hydraulics Laboratory can produce a 'perfect' wave in a test tank and then generate random waves to portray the real scene more accurately. But engineers do not have advice for a boardrider who finds himself in a difficult position in big seas off the Sunshine Coast *(left)*. They do have the facility though to record wave action off the coast monitoring even small movements of anchored wave riding buoys. Sunset over the Maroochy River *(left)* presents a placid scene but natural phenomena ensure this is not always so.

Concrete, bitumen and bricks have replaced or at least covered the sands that used to give a casual nature to Hastings Street, the main street of Noosa Heads. Old visitors criticise changes which have seen buildings like the Sheraton Noosa Heads (**above**) rise in place of others familiar over the years, and the landscaping for picnic grounds of the end-of-street camping ground, once a favourite holiday destination midway between beach and riverfront. Such are the demands of popularity. Shops and arcades now occupy what were the convenient backyards of beachfront guesthouses and the under-house parking areas of riverfront properties (**opposite middle**). For better or for worse, Hastings Street can hardly grow larger, but the brick footpaths will be needed for the ever-growing number of visitors to this most popular Sunshine Coast destination.

Fortunately, land planners of the last century were not all blind to the natural features of this landscape. The rugged and densely-forested headland at Noosa was set aside as a reserve long before the days of the 1930s when a bridge gave access to vehicles for the first time. The setting aside of more than 450 hectares of the headland as national park gives total protection to its landscape, plants and animals. Tea Tree Bay and Granite Bay on the park's northern frontage (**bottom**) are generally calm and inviting, so inviting the walking tracks have to be hardened to cope with intense visitation. Several areas of the forested, rugged slopes of the Blackall Range in the Mary Valley are also national park (**right**).

Severe erosion in the last few decades has seriously affected the extent of the beach at Noosa Heads but not its popularity (**opposite top**). Rock walls had to be built to protect valuable properties behind the beach, and groynes were erected to try to trap shifting sands. Authorities are still hopeful that one day Noosa will regain a broad beach and swimmers will again have rollers on which to surf to shore. Meanwhile, keen boardriders will still swear that the swell rounding Noosa Head and sweeping into Granite Bay in certain conditions provides one of the best 'waves' for boardriding in eastern Australia. The sheltered waters of the lower Noosa River provide safe anchorages for many boats including hire houseboats (**left**). This is the base for many tourist and houseboat cruises upriver into Lakes Cooribah and Cootharaba, Boreen Point, and beyond to Elanda Point, the over-water Kinaba information centre and Cooloola National Park. The park protects the catchment of the Upper Noosa River and extends to the beachfront and north to Rainbow Beach. The tide-free upstream reaches are ideal for sedate boating, or canoeing and camping if you are keen. Rock fishing is an art form practised by a few keen exponents at several rocky points along the Sunshine Coast including this spot opposite Mudjimba (Old Woman Island) off Maroochydore (**above**).

Toowoomba, 130 kilometres west of Brisbane, is known as the Queen City of the Darling Downs or Garden City, depending on your point of view. It's the business centre of the rich, rural areas of the sprawling Darling Downs and gateway to horse studs and sheep and cattle properties. As the second name implies, Toowoomba residents have complemented a community effort of providing public gardens by maintaining their own gardens. The annual spring Carnival of Flowers each September features a large home garden competition and a flower-theme procession. The city has many outstanding residences which reflect the region's wealth and gardening endeavour (**right**). Many also have chimneys for fireplaces, used on winter nights for Toowoomba has many more cooler nights than places on the coastal plain a few kilometres down the range. Toowoomba's parks and gardens also have playground equipment including former steam-powered tractors, rollers and locomotives as well has more traditional swings and hurdy gurdys (**opposite top**).

Rich dark soils and regular rainfall make for efficient farming on the Darling Downs and in the adjacent Lockyer Valley area. The Downs is noted for its hard wheat and other grain production. The Lockyer produces prime vegetables and root crops, maize and fodder. Yet farmers have been criticised for over-use of a valuable resource and warned that its productivity is threatened within a generation or two. Farming practices are under review, particularly those related to erosion prevention. The direction and extent of ploughing on the slopes and flats and retention and replanting of vegetation along watercourses and ridges are important aspects (**left**). Like similar crops the world over, sunflowers point their heads in the one direction (**below left**). This crop thrived by the New England Highway between Toowoomba and Warwick. Hereford cattle fatten well on the stubble of other crops like lucerne, grown under irrigation in the Lockyer Valley around Gatton (**below**).

Undulating Downs country between Toowoomba and Warwick (**above**). Wheatfields are grazed and left fallow before reploughing and replanting. This is 'winter wheat' country where a crop can be planted when the ground is sufficiently moist. Frosts are occasional and do not destroy young plants. Harvesting is usually completed in November before summer storm rains. Blaze of colour in Queens Park, Toowoomba, in September in time for the Carnival of Flowers (**right**).

Warwick is a small city on the southern Darling Downs, notable for the wealth of its surrounds, old buildings and history, and schools. Queensland's first free settlers came here in 1840. The restored Criterion Hotel (**bottom left**), reflects a style of architecture in vogue well before its 1917 completion date. Warwick is on one of the main interstate road transport routes between Brisbane and southern capitals. Even today, powerful transports sometimes have difficulty in negotiating the steep road through Cunningham's Gap in the Great Dividing Range (**below**). Broad-brimmed cowboy style hats are on sale in Warwick (**bottom**), a reminder that Warwick is more rural than urban and the fact that the city is home to the Warwick Rodeo each October.

Paddock of sorghum comes to head on a farm in the Lockyer Valley (**above**). Fertile soils and reliable underground water make the district one of the richest farming areas in Queensland. Lockyer potatoes, onions and pumpkins fetch top prices on local and interstate markets. Crops like peas and corn are sought by food companies for on-the-spot processing and freezing. Few people realise that the Lockyer is part of the Brisbane River catchment. Picnic Point, Toowoomba, is more than its name implies. It is a high point on the Great Dividing Range at Toowoomba with an outlook over the Moreton Region to Brisbane and beyond on a clear day (**right**). It is also one of several major parks along the over the edge of the range at Toowoomba, and a popular stopping point for travellers using the Warrego Highway from Brisbane west.

The lowest dip in the skyline Great Dividing Range (**below**) marks Cunningham's Gap, vital to a main thoroughfare between Brisbane and the inland, as it was when located by explorer Allan Cunningham in 1827. Its forested surrounds are part of Main Range National Park.

Pacific Ocean rollers expend their force on Frenchman's Beach, Point Lookout, as seen from the Cook Memorial (**below**). This is part of a superb wilderness area for many people for the Bay's surrounds are kept in their natural condition and access is denied to all but keen walkers.

Moreton Island is a very special part of Brisbane. It is another world away, on the opposite side of Moreton Bay. The growth of the townships of Kooringal, Bulwer and Cowan along with the Tangalooma resort are a direct outcome of enlarged vehicular ferry services from Scarborough to Bulwer and from Lytton to Kooringal in the last decade. Four-wheel-drive vehicles and passengers pour off the ferries and scatter over the island every weekend and holidays putting unprecedented pressures on Moreton's natural values. Authorities concerned with these (the island is more than 90 percent national park) have long argued for a suitable outcome and this seems to be in place with the 1991 declaration of the island as a recreation area. Fees are now payable for vehicle access and camping thus raising funds for the island's effective management and to provide facilities for visitors. Public input to a five-year management plan is certain to confirm the direction that Moreton should be conserved

in its present state with development restricted to the existing townships. Many aspire and perspire to reach the top of Mt Tempest, the island's highest point and reputed to be the highest windblown sandhill in the world. The early morning view over Moreton's open forests (**below**) is easily worth the perspiration. The Wrecks north of Tangalooma (**bottom**) provides the only protection for small craft on the island's western side. Extension and consolidation of this man-made breakwater are proposed. Mottled green waters wash Moreton's western beachfront, as seen from Kooringal looking north to Shark Spit and beyond (**right top**). The white patch in mid-picture is The Desert, a natural vegetation-free area of sand. The Sandhills as seen from the north-west (**right middle**) are a feature of the island's Bay side. The Big Sandhills (**right bottom**) are wind-blown sands which almost cross the island from ocean beach to Bay.

*Sunset over the One Mile boat harbour at Dunwich on Stradbroke Island with Peel Island on the horizon (**top**). The jetty is adjacent to one of Queensland's most historic cemeteries. Blue-green waters of southern Moreton Bay looking from over Stradbroke Island to Peel Island and the mainland (**above**).*

Dunwich (**left**) was a quarantine station for early Queensland immigrants. Sadly, many who survived the rigours of a long journey from Europe died of disease within sight of the journey's end. Since the 1950s, Dunwich has been the centre of mineral sandmining operations and the main ferry terminal. Armies of soldier crabs are prominent among the scavengers of the sand flats off Myora and Dunwich at low tide (**below**). Broad sandbanks south of Amity Point on Stradbroke Island are revealed at low tide (**bottom**). Presence of five cent-sized holes indicates the presence of 'yabbies', a soft-shelled crustacean pumped out for fishing bait when the banks are covered at high tide.

Double deck vehicular and passenger ferry leaves Toondah Harbour, Cleveland, for Dunwich, Stradbroke Island (**above**). At the other end of the Bay, the sun sets also over the water for fishermen using the jetty at Bongaree, Bribie Island (**right**). Bird Island is a tenacious coral cay in Moreton Bay off Dunwich (**opposite top**) — tenacious for sometimes winds, waves and cross-currents seemed to attempt to erode it to pieces in a matter of a few hours. Yet its sparse casuarinas and hardy grasses seem to hold it together as a popular landing spot for yachties who can anchor with care close to its western shore (**opposite bottom**).

Jumpinpin is the name given to a break between North and South Stradbroke Islands. While there must always have been low sandhills prone to erosion, reputedly the detonation in the sandhills of explosives recovered from the wreck of the vessel Cambus Wallace offshore in 1896 led to a permanent incursion by the ocean. Several times since, there have been two breaks, the most recent closing in 1988. Sandbanks in the area are subject to frequent change with weather and tidal conditions. Boating channels are not marked and are known only to regular users. These probably total several thousand since the Jumpinpin area along the Swan Bay, Kalinga Bank and the Pigsties end of North Stradbroke Island and adjacent waters are one of the most popular fishing areas in southern Queensland. Low tide reveals the shallows, the narrow channels of Jumpinpin with North Stradbroke in the distance, and also the proximity of ocean waves which can overturn the boats of the unwary (**left**).

Glassy waters of Horseshoe Bay off Peel Island (*above*), destination of many a boat and yacht in Moreton Bay for its mostly clear, clean waters over coral and sand, fine swimming at high tide, and even for a spot of keel diving inspection and hull scrubbing.

Visitors to such a large sprawling city as Brisbane are often surprised to find some rural atmosphere remains in its outer suburbs or adjoining areas. Look hard within the city boundary and one can still find cows being milked, horses and cattle tended, chickens raised, and fruit and vegetables grown commercially. Prawn and fishing trawlers work Moreton Bay and the Brisbane River, crabs are caught, and oysters are harvested off Moreton Island. The Samford Valley in the Pine Shire less than 30 minutes' drive north-west of Brisbane has been subdivided into fairly large lots (**above**). This has come about with the construction of the North Pine Dam and the flooding of the valley by Lake Samsonvale as a water storage. The North Pine Dam, Somerset Dam on the Stanley River (**opposite top**) and the Wivenhoe Dam on the Brisbane River are the region's main sources of domestic water.

Macleay Island in southern Moreton Bay remains largely a mangrove-fringed open forested retreat for a few commuters and retirees (**below**) but extensive subdivision, water and electricity services, and faster transport to and from the mainland could threaten its relative tranquillity soon. Plans to construct a bridge to nearby Russell Island and then to Stradbroke Island have been shelved for a decade. No such threat hangs over Mud Island in the middle of Moreton Bay (**bottom**). Its rubble beaches and mangrove channels appear certain to remain the preserve of private boatowners seeking its shelter from south-east winds and making an occasional visit ashore.

*Dusk over central Brisbane finds a cyclist wending his way home along the Toowong bikeway (**below**), apparently oblivious to the glassy surface of the Brisbane River reflecting some of the city's tallest structures. Behind the cyclist is the Merivale Street railway bridge, stretching from South Brisbane's tree-lined Riverside Drive.*

To claim that Brisbane has grown to a cosmopolitan city reflecting influences of many countries of the Eurasian and American continents, of Pacific neighbours and even other Australian states would be wrong. The population of the Brisbane region may be approaching 1 million but many residents consider it still should be likened to a big country town rather than an international city. This should come as no surprise for free European settlement in Queensland is not 150 years old, a matter of a few generations. Its lifestyle is basically conservative — people tend not to move far from 'home' and might remain in one place for decades. It's still possible to walk down Queen Street and bump into an old school friend or at least get a nod from a past business acquaintance. Queensland might be the most decentralised state in Australia but Brisbane is still 'the big smoke' where many country and provincial residents tend to visit every few years or so for one excuse or another like family reunions, industry or business conferences or simply to look! The answer to this enigma could lie with the city's weather and its lifestyle. One cannot be separated from the other. Not surprisingly, Brisbane enjoys a sub-tropical climate — generally warm days for much of the year with a few scorchers in summer and a few cold nights and mornings in winter. Unlike most Australian capitals, rainy days are in January-April and so are often pleasant respites. The June-August months often bring bitingly dry westerly winds but their effect is diminished by an outlook of sunny, cloudless skies. Honest Brisbaneites will confide they are drawn to the city and remain because of that climatic pattern. Such an environment encourages outdoor activities all the year, in fact requiring a conscious effort to participate in functions and events indoors. This is reinforced in summer with one hour's daylight saving between October and February. This gives residents and visitors cooler, early rises but an extra hour of sunshine at the end of the day, in a sense an artificial twilight. There's always the temptation to cool off in summer's heat swimming in a pool or at the beach, and take part in or watch more strenuous activities in winter. From the local school carnival to the Royal National Agricultural and Industrial Association's Show at Bowen Hills in August (the Ekka), from bream fishing to the football finals, from archery and bowls to cross-country running and yachting, there's never an off-peak time for something interesting to do and see in and around the city. The long-running Warana Festival has featured the year's most colourful and varied street procession with many marching bands to keep watching crowds up with the beat (**right**). At the Greek Community's Paniyiri Festival in Musgrave Park, South Brisbane (**top right**), there's no shortage of would-be Greek dancers with plenty of exponents, local-born and migrants, to help show them the techniques.

LIFESTYLES

Double skull rowers find the river's Town Reach a suitable place to train for regular regattas (**right**). At Comboyuro Point, Moreton Island, keen fishermen find their peace casting into the surf as the sun sets over the mainland (**below**). Only at Ekka time can a youthful visitor make a selection from so many helium-filled balloons (**bottom left**). While surf lifesavers no longer use four-oared boats for rescues, they keep their skills for competitive carnivals (**bottom right**).

Often in Brisbane, the test of personal fitness is to name those activities in which you have taken part to one degree or another in recent years. When you seem to have been exposed to them all, possibly as a spectator or media watcher, along comes another, often very strenuous. While facilities for many activities, particularly those in the outdoors, have been provided, relatively few people are active, regular participants. Many a suburban park now features part of a cross-suburbs bicycle trail but often pedestrians can use such trails without fear of having to jump aside for an errant, inexperienced cyclist! Safety-helmeted family groups with Junior riding 'training wheels' compete for space on the relatively narrow trails with enthusiastic, well-equipped wheelers out for an early morning fitness pedal of many kilometres (**left**). Sailboard riders come from all over the city to the shores of Moreton Bay at Rose Bay, Manly (**below left**), to test themselves and their colourful craft in all manner of breezes to gale force. Sponsored marathon sailboarding events have become very popular. The Brisbane City Council-sponsored FREEPS (Free recreation and entertainment for everyone in the parks) at city and suburban venues on many Sundays of the year have a wide range of spectators, as at the City Botanic Gardens (**below**).

The Royal National Association's annual show at the Exhibition Ground, Bowen Hills, has been a feature of Brisbane's lifestyle for more than a century. The 'Ekka' is staged over 10 days and nine nights in early August. Its packed variety attracts the greatest number of people on a population basis any Australian capital city show. These days, the industrial and commercial enterprises of the city vie with the natural wealth of the country represented particularly by merino sheep with the world's finest wool, and beef and dairy cattle. The main show ring has a non-stop program featuring equestrian events, sheep dog trials (where dogs are required to shepherd and finally pen three sheep while directed only by the owner's whistles), trotting races and rodeo events. Prize livestock head two grand parades. Timber-getter shows his determination in a cross-cut sawing competition in the woodchopping arena (**top left**). Sideshow Alley, an often-curious mixture of amusements, rides, and tests of skill, is an Ekka feature, and includes stalls selling dolls on walking sticks (**middle left**), dodgem car rides (**bottom left**), haunted house 'creatures' (**left**), and parachute rides (**right**), all in the shadow of a giant ferris wheel (**above**).

Once a week or once a year, there's always some number of Brisbaneites and visitors ready to enjoy aspects of the city's lifestyle, particularly those out of doors and in the sunshine. 'Paddy McGinnty's goat', complete with floral garland and in the safe care of a bearded owner may be an odd but not unusual participant in the city's Warana Procession (**above**). The sunshine is often so intense that rows of colourful umbrellas have become a trademark of the city's Sunday Riverside Markets, at least for many stallholders (**above right**). Others have products which can get wet when the occasional shower passes over. A shiny colourful balloon is more than enough to meet the need of a youthful visitor to the Markets (**right**).

Like the people of any modern city, Brisbaneites could not be said to be overly generous, except at times of natural disaster and extreme want by the least wealthy. So more than a great deal of effort is done by organisers of events to benefit charity to get people to take their hands out of their pockets to open their purses and wallets. For at least a decade, an unusual event on the fringe of the inner city has become a regular benefactor of city charities. This is the Spring Hill Fair, the place to be and be seen on a weekend in springtime. Stalls selling food, drinks, clothing, trinkets and innumerable other things are set up on streets in a block bounded by Wickham Terrace and Leichhardt Street in the inner suburb of Spring Hill. In Brisbane's first century, this was a fashionable residential area being only a brisk walk or buggy ride from the central city business area. In the last decade, the Brisbane City Council has made several efforts to ensure that what remains of this residential heritage is continued in a precinct without immediate of threat of demolition for replacement by high rises and town house blocks. Its most famous elderly resident is antiques dealer Cecilia McNally, the 'dame' of Spring Hill. The Fair was her idea and she still plays a major part in its organisation each year. A typical Fair has stalls of herbs and other plants growing from hand-made pots (**top left**), plenty of shoppers for clothes and craftware (**middle left**), topped with burgers and beans (**below left**). Clowns and children (**above**) add to the atmosphere.

Water provides a challenging difference to Brisbane lifestyle. The proximity of the river and the vast Moreton Bay entices use from tiny sabots to large cruisers and ocean-going yachts. The sheltered waters of many of the city reaches of the river are used by schoolboys, men and women for rowing training either at dawn or dusk. The Commercial Rowing Club's pontoon and clubhouse at South Brisbane are often busy as all manner of craft and their users come and go (**below**). Few other places can offer such a facility within a 10-minute walking range of work. Horseshoe Bay in the southern side of Peel Island in Moreton Bay is a popular destination for a day or weekend cruise or sail (**right**). On such a glassy day, the water is often clear giving a view to the coral sand bottom. Development on the island has been avoided so Peel can provide an unspoilt wilderness landscape feeling for tired city dwellers. Many of the Bay's vessels are stored in safety in marina pens of the Manly boat harbour (**below right**).

Abseiling, or descending down rock faces using ropes, is another activity for the keen and the active within a few minutes' drive of the central city. Here on the cliffs of Kangaroo Point with the Story Bridge, the river and the city skyline in the background two enthusiasts begin a controlled descent (**above**). While such rock work always has some danger, the rock surface here is firm and dry. The cliffs are a convenient practice area for more formidable climbs and descents at the renowned Glasshouse Mountains to Brisbane's north and Mounts Barney and French to the south. Skills and energy of a different sort are required for board sailing. The Waterloo Bay section of Moreton Bay is a popular venue, particularly for sailors operating out of Wellington Point (**left**). This is a narrow isthmus providing good takeoff for winds from any quarter.

Brisbane's climate is conducive to most sports and pastimes except those requiring snow and ice. While 'summer' sports such as cricket can be washed out by regular rains and storms, 'winter' sports such as four codes of football are rarely disrupted. But even here, fishermen are like fishermen the world over. They can still find an excuse in the wind, the water or the weather generally for poor catches.

The Brisbane Broncos wear the gold and maroon jerseys with distinction (*above*). The Broncos is the premier Queensland team in the New South Wales rugby league top professional competition and is assured of sellout crowds when play is in Brisbane. Game fishing off Cape Moreton (*above right*) is a highly technical and demanding pastime that, with some luck, has resulted in numerous national and international record catches over the years. Kayaking on Lake Manchester, part of Brisbane's water supply operation, is a more sedate pastime (*middle right*). Ballymore Oval at Herston is the home of the amateur rugby union code in Queensland, and scene of many national and international rugby clashes. (*right*)

The amount of equipment needed to participate in a chosen activity of course varies widely. 'Queensland Maid' (**below**) is a locally-owned 'pocket maxi' yacht requiring many dollars and many hands and muscles to keep it competitive in world-class yachting events in Australian waters such as the Sydney-Hobart Yacht Race. The Victoria Park Golf Course at Herston (**right**) is another facility within a few minutes' drive of the inner city. It is adjacent to the Royal Brisbane Hospital complex, and has the central city is another skyline feature. Brisbane City Council involvement ensures the course is open to the public, even on busy weekends. The outer suburbs of Moggill, Pullenvale and Brookfield have special areas for equestrian events including show jumping (**below right**).

Fortunately, while strong winds can whip up rough seas on Moreton Bay at times, often conditions are near calm, particularly at night and in the morning. Do not believe the yachtie or boatie who tells tales of being harbour-bound by the weather for weekend after weekend. It only seems that way at times. Between Peel Island and Dunwich on Stradbroke Island is a mere speck, called Bird Island. At high tide, even large boats can anchor within a few metres of shore to let passengers regain their land legs briefly on the coral rubble sand and to have a swim (**above left**). A few casuarinas and other salt-resistant plants are its only vegetation. As the environmental park island is no more than a metre above high tide mark, its shape and surface are subject to rapid change in certain weather and tide conditions. Adjacent waters pose few hazards and are popular venues for trailer-sailer yachting events, some serious, often quite casual (**below left**). The casuarina-fringed foreshore at Horseshoe Bay, Peel Island, is a tempting place for overnight camping for runabout owners (**above**) but many a boatie has come to grief here when a fresh wind has sprung up from the south.

Brisbane's lifestyle is hardly static. While for example the City Botanic Gardens may have been in place for more than 135 years, even a local can never be sure whether a change is a one-off special or a new permanent feature. Scenes on these pages make the point. Strings of coloured lights give a new dimension to the trunks, branches and foliage of Gardens trees at night (*far left, top*). Seafood, champagne and a good view make for a pleasant riverside restaurant meal (*far left, below*). Umbrella-shaded tables are used by Gardens diners (*opposite, top*) while young spectators choose to sit in the sun there to enjoy a laugh with a clown (*opposite, below*). Train without rails takes Warana contest entrants along Adelaide Street (*left*), while hay bales help give flavour to a country-western theme float (*below left*). Visiting Japanese percussion group brings a new sound to King George Square (*below*).

Many of the pastimes of residents in the Brisbane region are on or beside river, Bay or ocean waters. Playing in the sand is an age-old tradition of children, here continued at Sandgate (**below**). Board paddler struggles to maintain direction in the face of a dumping wave in shallow water (**right**). Cub scouts wearing essential lifejackets, hats and sunburn cream take to canoes with qualified instructors to cross Cabbage Tree Creek from the Scout Association's Brownsea water activities centre, Shorncliffe (**below right**).

End of the day and the return to port is time for pictures of the ones that did not get away. An unusual dolphin fish is the subject of this scene on the rear deck of a Brisbane-based game fishing launch (**left**). Tanned lifesavers listen to their surfboat captain after a training row out through the breakers and back at a near Brisbane beach (**below left**). Many lifesavers give up every weekend in the summer season to the cause of surf safety. Pumicestone Passage between Bribie Island and the mainland at the northern end of Moreton Bay is a favoured spot for fishing (**below**). Much of its mangrove fringes are in a national park and so habitats and food sources for the 'big ones' are assured here.

A line extending from the Shorncliffe Pier is the starting point for Queensland's premier blue water yachting classic, the Brisbane to Gladstone ocean yacht race (**left**). Every Easter since 1947, the 307-nautical mile race has attracted many top racing and cruising yachts vying for The Courier-Mail trophy. While much public kudos is directed to the first yacht across the line, yachtie honours go to the boat and crew winning on handicap for they have sailed the best. Some entrants have been becalmed and taken more than a week to finish. A race for multi-hulled yachts held over a similar route has seen top boats reach Gladstone within 24 hours of the start.

Day and night, indoors and out, there's never a lull in the endless stream of things to do and see in and around Brisbane. Newspaper entertainment columns and weekly pastime liftouts are filled with suggestions for those finding or making time. The broadsheet pages of Brisbane's morning newspaper, The Courier-Mail, can also be handy for shade when the sun becomes too warm (**right**). The City Botanic Gardens is not only for possums and fruit bats at night. Citizens are attracted by entertainment as diverse as male choirs (**below**), rock concerts, classic film screenings and Christmas story-telling on the river stage. Free music events from individual performances to symphony orchestras have been offered in Brisbane for 50 years. Once a year for three days the main auditorium of the City Hall is transformed into a massive flower garden (**middle right**). This is the Chelsea Flower Show to aid the Red Cross, a Queensland version of the famous London event. The Warana procession always has contrast — from colourful children's promotions (**below left**) to the original uniforms of mounted infantry re-enactment groups (**below right**).

Demands of Australian football in kicking and running show in the action snap of a Brisbane Bears player (**left**). Compare the sleeveless jersey with those worn in other football codes. The Bears take their name from the city but play many of their Australian Football League competition matches on the Gold Coast. The Brisbane Bullets is another professional sporting team taking its name from the city. In the last decade, basketball has gained an army of keen followers and viewers. The Boondall Entertainment Centre is packed for matches when the Bullets compete (**below left**). The Spring Hill Fair demands a different athleticism for its patrons are required to walk up and down steep streets like Birley and Berry Streets (**below**).

Walking tracks and graded firebreaks of Brisbane Forest Park attract many keen walkers from Brisbane (**above**) for this large natural area is on the city's back doorstep. In the last decade, Bellbird Grove and Ironbark Gully picnic and recreation areas have joined national park areas such as Jolly's Lookout (named after Brisbane's first Lord Mayor) as get-away-from-it-all places for a few hours or a day. Cycling is not so demanding on the legs along the Manly boat harbour esplanade and there's no traffic either (**top right**). The Mayfair Crest Hotel opposite the City Hall has an open-air rooftop swimming pool (**below right**) which used to be a secluded, relaxing hideaway for guests until taller office blocks were built nearby.

The Brisbane City Council's pool complex at Chandler is world class providing opportunities for many people from those undertaking medical therapy to water polo players to many swimming champions. At times, there are even learn-to-kayak classes (**above left**). Gone are the days when Brisbane's parks had only a few chain and splintery hardwood plank or old tyre swings. Today, many cater for younger visitors by providing challenging but safe equipment in modern materials and bright colours as well as sandpits and other play areas (**left**). At the end of the day (or even in the middle after the sun has risen over the yardarm!), the Brisbane lifestyle is such that there is always a shady place nearby for a drink or two, a chat, and something to eat. Garden settings such as this one off Caxton Street, Petrie Terrace (**above**), have helped change the old image of Brisbane hotels as places only for beer-swilling, stubby and thong-wearing, loud mouthed 'yobbos'. You may now do business and enjoy pleasant surroundings and company for the cost of only a round or two of drinks. Is there any place to be other than Brisbane for such a relaxing lifestyle?

St Helena Island in Moreton Bay looking towards the Brisbane River mouth with the city beyond (**below**). St Helena, Fort Lytton, Moreton Island and Jolly's Lookout are the four national parks within the Brisbane City boundary. The island preserves the remains of Queensland's major jail from 1867 to 1932.

Today's landscape includes trees planted to make warders' gardens and an olive plantation. The chief warder's cottage has been restored and relics uncovered and returned to St Helena are on view. Despite its sometimes grim history, St Helena is an integral part of Brisbane's and Queensland's social and cultural history.

Rainbow lorikeet pauses on the rim of a hollow tree limb, often a desirable place in which to build a concealed nest (**right**). 'Lory's' and 'greenies' (scaly-breasted lorikeets) are familiar birds to many Brisbane residents for they often reside in the suburbs in numbers. In seeking nectar in the suburbs, lorikeets will perform all sorts of acrobatics grasping the thinnest branches of flowering trees and shrubs. They are a playful, likeable bird if a noisy one. They screech and chatter incessantly as they feed, taking a particular liking to the red flower stalks of umbrella trees. While it's not hard to get them to feed from bowls of watered-down honey, wildlife authorities recommend against regular feeding of all birds because this makes them too dependant and their numbers can upset an already strained balance of species in suburban backyards. Aviary escapes are blamed for flocks of sulphur-crested cockatoos and galahs in the Brisbane area when their normal habitat is in the inland. Ferns grow profusely in the shade of melaleuca trees in the Nudgee Waterhole reserve (**below**). This is a 19 hectare reserve, the smallest of several wetlands in Brisbane's north. The waterhole is covered by reeds and sedges and surrounded by mixed forest with Queensland bluegum. The Boondall wetlands further along the Gateway arterial road are similar in appearance with mangroves fringing areas inundated by tidal waters several times a year. The Brisbane City Council plans to retain most of this area while approving a limited shopping complex.

Kangaroos may be seen and even patted and fed in numerous zoos and tourist ventures in and around Brisbane (**left**). While the animal is a symbol of Australia, in good conditions it is a prolific breeder and zoo keepers are becoming more reluctant to keep many. Visitors and Brisbaneites are surprised to learn that kangaroos or more particularly their smaller relatives the wallabies may be seen in the wild around Brisbane. The agile, whiptail, red-necked and swamp wallabies are said to be common in bush habitats. Smaller pademelons may be seen feeding of grassy verges of Brisbane Forest Park rainforests. A bright golden version of the dark grey to black swamp wallaby is found only on Stradbroke Island. The kookaburra (or laughing jackass) (**centre left**) is Brisbane's most commonly reported bird and is found throughout except in the inner city. Its large beak and firm gaze are identifiable features if its 'laughing' call has not been heard in advance. Many residents feed kookaburras regularly and develop a special liking for 'their' birds but this is not shared by other birds whose nestlings they take. For this reason, kookaburras are often the target of other suburban birds like noisy miners, willie wagtails and peewees (magpie larks). The black flying-fox may be seen in closeup at Fleay's Fauna Centre at West Burleigh on the Gold Coast (**below**). This is not a fox but the largest of the fruit bats, found in growing numbers in all 'camps' around Brisbane.

*A gourmet would be quick to identify the picture (**below**) as a symbol of Queensland. Instantly recognized are cooked tiger prawns ready to eat, a blue swimmer crab (red when cooked), and a trussed fresh Queensland mudcrab ready for cooking (when it turns red also).*

A city such as Brisbane simply does not happen. One million people in the region cannot survive by living hand to mouth from backyard fruit and vegetable gardens and by bartering. Commerce, education, government and exports provide many jobs but it's industry that provides a strong basis for any economy. Brisbane as Queensland's capital and main port has long been the centre for industry in the state. Improved transport and communications are factors that have brought great change to industry in Brisbane, particularly in the last decade or so. Ship building and ship repair facilities and engineering works have closed. Port activities have contracted downriver to Hamilton and the river mouth. Factories and warehouses in the city, Valley and South Brisbane areas have either closed or moved. At the same time, business has flourished in the suburbs closer to demand. Coopers Plains, Acacia Ridge, Archerfield, Rocklea and Wacol are now the southside industrial areas. Geebung, Zillmere and Banyo are busy northside areas. Enoggera, Bulimba, Stafford and Hemmant are among a score of other suburbs with concentrations of industry. Business is generally small. Plants like the South Brisbane glassworks, the Castlemaine Perkins brewery at Milton, the Ford assembly plant at Eagle Farm, the Volvo truck and bus factory at Wacol and two oil refineries are now the exceptions to what was the Brisbane large-plant perspective. Light industry covers an unexpectedly wide range from the usual manufacture, maintenance and building construction business to processing prawns for export and design and production of quality electronics for satellites. Recycling of glass, metals and paper and other resources is becoming a more attractive proposition for industry. Environmental standards are observed generally by industry. The days of belching smokestacks over Brisbane are past and waste minimisation is industry's direction in the 1990s. More attention is being given to occupational health and safety issues to benefit workers and industry. Hardhats and boots are musts for everyone on worksites (**right**). Containerisation of cargo has brought new dockside work practices and faster turnarounds for ships entering Brisbane (**above right**).

INDUSTRY

Feeding a large demanding population is a major task for primary and secondary industries in and around Brisbane. Alas, the days of the Redlands 'salad bowl' are numbered as housing overtakes some of the region's prime farming soils in the same way as the urban sprawl has taken over Sunnybank more than a decade ago. Prime tomatoes, strawberries, avocadoes and custard apples grown in the Redland Bay district (**top right**) find ready buyers at the Brisbane Markets at Rocklea or are sent to southern capitals. Fresh milk is another product in demand. Road tankers bring thousands of litres to processing and packaging plants in and around Brisbane. Milk is delivered to homes in most Brisbane suburbs six days a week. The region's climate is the best in Australia for raising meat chickens. These go to market at an average age of 45 days and weighing 1.8 kilograms. Processing plants at Wulkuraka, Park Ridge and Murarrie meet the demands for millions of birds, these days mostly for the fresh meat market. Queensland produces much of Australia's cotton crop and this is partly processed at a Brisbane ginnery before export interstate or overseas (**right**). Wacol Industrial Estate has been a major initiative by the Queensland Government in recent years. The estate has provided facilities including a railway siding to bring together industries otherwise seeking limited urban space. Production Street, Progress Road and Industrial Avenue have become the addresses of many prominent industrial firms. Landscaping has removed the otherwise often rugged appearance of industrial premises at Wacol (**below**).

Swanbank Power Station on the south-eastern outskirts of Ipswich (**above**) was once the prime source of electricity for the south-east Queensland grid and therefore of vital importance to industry in the region. It used coal from local underground mines. The coming on-line of the massive Tarong power station near Nanango using open cut coal has eased the demand on Swanbank but its output is still essential at peak loading times in winter. Its water storage ponds have become known as a favourite bird-watching area in the Ipswich district. In recent years, the beer brewing enterprises of Castlemaine Fourex and Carlton in Brisbane have been attacked by a newcomer, Powers (**left**). Products from its new brewery at Yatala, about halfway between Brisbane the Gold Coast, have taken a more than expected share of a valuable market. The Beenleigh distillery on the Albert River at Yatala has long been known for its pot-still rum made from juice of locally crushed sugar cane.

Trawler returns to its base in Cabbage Tree Creek, Shorncliffe, after a night trawling for prawns in Moreton Bay *(below)*. The Bay is probably the most important maritime resource along the Queensland coast for it is the approach to the Port of Brisbane, a very prolific commercial fishery, and an outstanding area for water-based recreation. The Queensland Government's Moreton Bay Strategic Plan seeks to balance competing uses by proposing a zoning system for uses. In this way, the fishing industry would be protected and areas set aside for conservation and fish breeding. A suitable number of trawlers would be allowed to operate between Sunday and Friday nights. Weekends would be exclusively recreation apart from ferry transport to the islands. The supply, storage and maintenance of pleasure craft using Moreton Bay has become a large industry in itself worth many millions of dollars to the economy each year.

The Ford Motor Company's Brisbane assembly plant at Eagle Farm has been providing specialised engine and car assembly jobs for many years (**left**). Ford remained in Brisbane after General Motors-Holden closed down its Acacia Ridge plant. Golden sand is returned to Stradbroke Island after the extraction of the 'minerals sands' of titanium, rutile, zircon and monazite (**below**). A powerful dredge floating in a moving pond is used to extract the valuable products which are taken to the mainland from Dunwich before export. Sand mining companies are making great efforts to rehabilitate mined areas to their near natural shape and to encourage regrowth of local native species. Conservation interests have sought to strictly limit or to close down sandmining in the rich southern Queensland coastal sand areas. Sand has been mined continuously on Stradbroke Island for more than 40 years and leases have been granted to cover at least another 10 years.

Valuable catch of prawns freshly cooked and ready for baskets for sales coming off a trawler in Cabbage Tree Creek (**left**). Radar and colour echo sounders are used by experienced skippers with care to ensure they can continue to take the best mature prawns from Bay waters and not threaten the fishery by trawling too close to inshore nursery areas. Most prawn trawling is done at night. The Fisherman Islands shipping terminals at the mouth of the Brisbane River (**below left** and **centre**) have revolutionised cargo handling in Brisbane. A large swing basin means that large ships with deep drafts can now have access to container terminals and heavy lift cranes. Wharves and cargo areas were constructed from reclaimed land in a project designed to return large ships to the port after dredging failed to keep river channels deep after the 1974 floods. Bulk cargoes including coal can be handled at adjacent terminals. The Moreton Bay plan allows for expansion of Fisherman Islands wharves to include Bishop Island, an island constructed entirely of mud and sand dredged from the Brisbane River. The Roma Street railway goods yard (**left**) is an anachronism from the 19th century when industry and markets were in or near central Brisbane. Several plans have called for their relocation to outer suburbs but action has been discontinued. Authorities are still considering a proposal for a casino to take over one corner of the railway yards area. Roma Street remains the major Brisbane station for the interstate passenger service to Sydney and for coastal services to Cairns.